Collins

INTERNATIONAL PRIMARY ENGLISH

Workbook 4

William Collins' dream of knowledge for all began with the publication of his first book in 1819.
A self-educated mill worker, he not only enriched millions of lives, but also founded a flourishing publishing house. Today, staying true to this spirit, Collins books are packed with inspiration, innovation and practical expertise. They place you at the centre of a world of possibility and give you exactly what you need to explore it.

Collins. Freedom to teach.

An imprint of HarperCollins*Publishers*
The News Building
1 London Bridge Street
London SE1 9GF

browse the complete Collins catalogue at
www.collins.co.uk

© HarperCollins*Publishers* Limited 2016

10 9 8 7

ISBN 978-0-00-814770-9

British Library Cataloguing in Publication Data
A catalogue record for this publication is available from the British Library.

Publisher Celia Wigley
Publishing manager Karen Jamieson
Commissioning editor Lucy Cooper
Series editor Karen Morrison
Managing editor Caroline Green
Editor Amanda Redstone
Project managed by Emily Hooton
Edited by Karen Williams
Proofread by Gaynor Spry and Cassie Fox
Cover design by Amparo Barrera
Cover artwork by Priyankar Gupta
Internal design by Ken Vail Graphic Design
Typesetting by Ken Vail Graphic Design and Jouve India Private Limited
Illustrations by Ken Vail Graphic Design, Priyankar Gupta, Advocate Art and Beehive Illustrations
Production by Robin Forrester

Printed and bound by Martins the Printers

Text acknowledgements
The publishers gratefully acknowledge the permissions granted to reproduce copyright material in the book. Every effort has been made to contact the holders of copyright material, but if any have been inadvertently overlooked, the Publisher will be pleased to make the necessary arrangements at the first opportunity.

HarperCollins*Publishers* Limited for an extract and artwork from *Let's Go to Mars* by Janice Marriott, illustrated by Mark Ruffle, text copyright © Janie Marriott; for an extract and artwork from *The Brave Baby* by Malachy Doyle, illustrated by Richard Johnson. Text reproduced by permission of HarperCollins*Publishers*; The Catchpole Agency. HarperCollins*Publishers* for an extract and artwork from *I've Just had a Bright Idea*, written and illustrated by Scoular Anderson, text copyright © Scoular Anderson; for an extract and artwork from *Peter and the Wolf* by Diane Redmond, illustrated by John Bendall-Brunello, text copyright © Diane Redmond. Text reproduced by permission of HarperCollins*Publishers*; Rosemary Sandberg.

David Higham Associates for an extract from "Street Child" by Berlie Doherty published in *Collins Primary Literacy Pupil Book 4*, pp.4-5. Reproduced with permission; Ann Webley for material adapted from *Collins Primary Literacy Pupil Book 4*, pp.50-51, 90. Reproduced with permission; David Higham Associates for the poems "Old Man Ocean" and "The Crow" by Russell Hoban published in *The Pedalling Man*, Heinemann, 1991 © The Trustees of the Russell Hoban Trust; Bloomsbury and Peters Fraser & Dunlop for the poems 'The Youngest' and 'Last One Into Bed' by Michael Rosen, published in *Mustard, Custard, Grumble Belly and Gravy*, Bloomsbury Publishing Plc. Reprinted by permission of Bloomsbury and Peters Fraser & Dunlop (www.petersfraserdunlop.com) on behalf of Michael Rosen; David Higham Associates for an extract from *Goggle Eyes* by Anne Fine, Penguin; and *Kamla and Kate* by Jamila Gavin, Mammoth. Reproduced with permission; First News for Schools for extracts from 'Malala's Award' and ' Mini Mars Mission', www.firstnews.co.uk. Reproduced with permission; Solo Syndication for an extract from "An Alien? Fat Chance!", *Daily Mail*, 14/01/1998, copyright © Solo Syndication, 1998; Irene Rawnsley for the poem "A Good Idea" published *in Dog's Dinner* by Irene Rawnsley, Methuen Children's Books, 1990. Reproduced by kind permission of the author; Chris Baker for an extract from *Sheetal's First Landing*, copyright © Chris Baker, 2015. Reproduced by kind permission of the author; Judith Nicholls for the poem "The Last Dragon" published in *Storm's Eye*, Oxford University Press; 1994, copyright © Judith Nicholls. Reproduced by kind permission of the author; Brian Moses for the poem "Lost Magic" published in *Behind the Staffroom Door*, Macmillan Children's Books, 2007. Reproduced by kind permission of the author; and George Szirtes for the poem "The bicycle's wrists" published in *In the Land of Giants*, Salt Publishing, 2012. Reproduced by kind permission of the author.

Photo acknowledgements
The publishers wish to thank the following for permission to reproduce photographs. Every effort has been made to trace copyright holders and to obtain their permission for the use of copyright materials. The publishers will gladly receive any information enabling them to rectify any error or omission at the first opportunity.

(t = top, c = centre, b = bottom, r = right, l = left)

Cover & p1 Priyankar Gupta
p1 Rosemary Woods/Collins, p4 stockshoppe/Shutterstock, p6 Lorelyn Medina/Shutterstock, p9 Matthew Cole/Shutterstock, p11 Aliaksei_Z/Shutterstock, p12 Ermolaev Alexander/Shutterstock, p13 John T Takai/Shutterstock, p17 Emeraldora/Shutterstock, p19 imageBROKER/Alamy, p20 pzAxe/Shutterstock, p21 VladimirCeresnak/Shutterstock, p25 b Matthew Cole/Shutterstock, p27 Matthew Cole/Shutterstock, p28 t Eric Isselee/Shutterstock, p28 b skylark art/Shutterstock, p29 Lorelyn Medina/Shutterstock, p30 t koya979/Shutterstock, p31 t fresher/Shutterstock, p31 b stockyimages/Shutterstock, p36 titosart/Shutterstock, p37 Jstone/Shutterstock, p38 Christian Vinces/Shutterstock, p39 Szasz-Fabian Jozsef/Shutterstock, p40 t Blambca/Shutterstock, p42 humphrey/Shutterstock, p52 Anton Brand/Shutterstock, p54 c iStock/ThinkStock.

Contents

1 Stories of the past

Reading Student's Book pages 2–3

1 Reread the extract from *Street Child* on pages 2 to 3 of the Student's Book. What do you think Barnie was thinking, as he stared into the fire? Write his thoughts in the thought bubble.

2 What kind of person is Barnie? Fill in the spider diagram with words and phrases to describe him.

What he looks like:

How he talks:

Barnie

What he does:

How he treats Jim:

Four good words to describe him:

Student's Book page 4

1 Fill in the missing parts of the verb 'to be' in the boxes below.

Present	Past	Future
I am	I _____	I _____
You _____	You were	You will be
She is	He _____	It _____
We _____	We were	We _____
They _____	They _____	They will be

2 Add the correct part of the verb *to be*, to complete each sentence below.

a Present: I _____ the fastest runner in my class.

b Present: Amira _____ my sister's best friend.

c Past: Dad _____ very good at maths when he _____ my age.

d Past: Jon's favourite meal _____ chicken stir-fry.

e Future: We _____ at Grandma's house this weekend.

f Future: Sahar says she _____ an astronaut when she grows up.

3 Sami is telling his friend what he did last weekend. Write what he is saying. Remember to use the past tense and don't forget punctuation!

Grammar | Student's Book page 5

1 Underline all the verbs in these sentences. Then rewrite each sentence, replacing the verbs with more powerful ones. The first one has been done for you.

- Jim <u>walked</u> slowly towards the market.

  Jim plodded slowly towards the market.

  _____

- Barnie looked at Jim.

  _____

- Meera spoke quietly.

  _____

- Stanley ran all the way home.

  _____

- James went upstairs.

  _____

2 Add speech marks to the sentences below, and fill the gaps with interesting words for 'said'. The first one has been done for you.

a "I'm sorry," *whispered* Alice.

b How dare you? _____ Mrs Sangheera.

c It's so exciting! _____ Matthew.

d Have you eaten your breakfast? _____ Mum.

e It's time for school! _____ Ella.

f I've got a sore throat, _____ Rajiv.

g We're going shopping this afternoon, _____ Michael.

h Don't let him hear you, _____ Selma.

i It's bedtime in five minutes, _____ Auntie Bess.

j Stop that at once! _____ Mr Taylor.

1 All the punctuation marks have dropped off these sentences! Write the sentences out again, and add the punctuation. You can use . , ? ! " "

a What do you want for lunch

_____

b I like playing football cricket and tennis

_____

c Look I can see a dragon

_____

d My sister loves going swimming

_____

e Miguel Tom Sam and Kieran are playing tag on the beach

_____

f Are we nearly there yet asked Molly

_____

g Look out or you'll crash

_____

2 Read these sentences, and write 'list' at the end if the commas are separating items in a list. Write 'clauses' if the commas are separating clauses.

    a I ate a samosa, a packet of peanuts, an apple and a banana. _____

    b Tuesday is my favourite day, because we have swimming lessons.

       _____

    c My three best friends are Natalia, Grace and Tom. _____

    d I live next door to Natalia, but Grace and Tom live on the other side

       of town. _____

    e Whenever I go to see Grandma, she gives me a cookie. _____

3 Add the missing commas in these sentences.

    a My favourite month is March mostly because that's when my birthday is.

    b Ahmed's new top has stripes of red green white and blue.

    c Ahmed wants to wear his top to play football but his mum might be cross if he gets it dirty.

    d If you want to see the new-born kittens come home with me after school.

    e The kittens' names are Mina Jake Harry and Snowball.

4 <u>Circle</u> the words in the sentences below that use the apostrophe correctly.

    a I found Michael's/Michaels'/Micha'els bag.

    b The children's/child'rens/childrens' bedroom was very messy.

    c The girls/girl's/girls' mouths were open in surprise.

    d The dragons'/dragon's/dra'gons/tail was long and scaly.

    e Grandad's/Grandads'/Gran'dads favourite chair is broken.

    f We could hear the sound of the womens'/women's/wom'ens voices.

    g My brothers'/brother's/brothers arm is broken.

    h The boys'/boys/boy's mothers came running.

Read these sentences with –ing and –ed verbs. If the verbs are spelt correctly, draw a circle round them. If they are spelt wrongly, write them correctly at the end of the line.

a   Lee is puting his football boots on. _____

b   Carlo cleanned up his room quickly before Mum saw it.

   _____

c   The old cat is sitting in the sunshine. _____

d   Shh! The baby is sleepping! _____

e   Grandad is digging in the garden. _____

f   I asked if I could have an extra slice of cake. _____

g   Jake had a lot of trouble findding his phone charger. _____

h   I've been working hard all day. _____

i   Poppy hoped from one foot to the other impatiently. _____

j   Asif stepped carefully across the thin wooden plank. _____

1 Read the start of this historical story. Choose a connective from the box to fill each of the gaps. You may need to use some of the connectives more than once.

or	however	and	because	but

Tom yawned _____ stretched sleepily. It was the start of his first day at Doctor Thomas Barnardo's home for destitute boys. Tom had come to the home the previous evening, _____ he had no food and nowhere to live. He knew that Doctor Barnardo would let him come in, _____ Doctor Barnardo was famous for his kindness to poor children. _____, Tom was nervous this morning. What would life in Doctor Barnardo's home be like? Would he fit in with the other boys, _____ would they make fun of him? Tom wanted to stay under the blankets a while longer, _____ he knew that he had to get up and face the day.

2 Write the next paragraph of the story. You can decide what happens! Try to use connectives in some of your sentences.

_____

_____

_____

_____

_____

3 Read the sentences below, and write an adjective to fill each gap.

a My baby sister loves her _____, _____ teddy bear.

b Mina has _____ hair and _____ eyes.

c Brandon's mum is very _____.

d I put on my coat because it was a _____ day.

e The monster had fourteen _____ eyes and a hundred _____ teeth.

4 Choose stronger adjectives to replace the underlined adjectives below. Use the words in the box to help you, if you like. Then rewrite the sentences including the stronger adjectives.

tiny	gigantic	freezing	boiling	young	ancient
ravenous	disgusting	full	terrifying	enormous	

a It was <u>cold</u>, and Marti's teeth chattered.

_____

b Ella pulled on an <u>old</u> T-shirt and went out to play.

_____

c Jamie was <u>hungry</u>, so he ate his sandwich.

_____

d It was <u>scary</u> being out alone in the dark.

_____

e Mariam saw a <u>small</u> kitten peeping out through the gate.

_____

2 Mars: the trip of a lifetime!

Reading Student's Book page 13

Read these facts about Mars. Draw a wavy line under any facts that make Mars sound like a good place to visit. Draw a circle round any facts that make Mars sound like a bad place to visit.

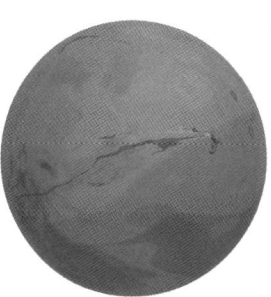

Would you like to go to Mars? Here are some Martian facts to help you make up your mind!

- Mars is Earth's next-door neighbour! Earth is the third planet from the Sun, and Mars is the fourth planet. But, even though they are neighbours in the Solar System, Earth and Mars are still about 225 million kilometres apart. It would take roughly 260 days to get from Earth to Mars.

- Mars is smaller, colder and dryer than Earth. The average temperature on Mars is -62°C. That's 62 degrees below freezing, which is colder than Earth's Arctic circle in the middle of winter!

- Mars is often called the Red Planet because of its red soil. The soil on Mars is red because it is rusty (it contains iron oxide).

- Mars's rusty, dusty soil is very dry indeed. Sometimes there are enormous dust storms on Mars – big enough to cover the whole planet!

- Even though the surface of Mars is so dry, scientists have discovered that there is lots of frozen water under the surface of the planet. This means that if people ever travelled to Mars, they might be able to get the water they need by extracting and melting the ice.

- The air on Mars is mostly carbon dioxide, which is poisonous to humans – so any visitors would definitely need a spacesuit to survive!

- There are lots of interesting things to see on Mars. The massive volcano called Olympus Mons is three times bigger than Everest – and it is probably the biggest volcano in the whole Solar System. There is also an enormous canyon on Mars that is nearly as long as the United States of America is wide! At night you would see not one, but two, moons rising in the sky.

Student's Book pages 14–16

1 Read the sentences below. Write F at the end of the facts, and O at the end of the opinions.

a   Mars would be a really fun place to visit. ☐

b   No human beings have ever yet gone to Mars. ☐

c   Mars is the fourth planet from the Sun. ☐

d   Mars is colder than Earth. ☐

e   Life on Earth is a lot more interesting than life on Mars. ☐

f   Mars has two moons. ☐

g   Nights on Mars are more beautiful than nights on Earth. ☐

h   It is too dangerous for humans to visit Mars. ☐

i   Humans need spacesuits to protect them if they visit Mars. ☐

j   The soil on Mars is a much nicer colour than the soil on Earth. ☐

2 Find an interesting fact about Mars, and write it here.

1 Underline the imperative verbs in the orders below.

a Drink your milk quickly – it's time to go to school.

b Look out for crocodiles!

c Put the flour in the mixing bowl.

d Open the window so we can get some fresh air.

e Jump over the fallen logs.

2 Change these questions into orders. The first one has been done for you.

a Are you coming swimming with us?

Come swimming with us.

b Could you help Mum get dinner ready?

_____

c Have you washed your hands?

_____

d Can you look after your sister?

_____

e Are you going to eat your rice?

_____

3 One of these children is asking a question and the other is giving an order. Write what they are saying in the speech bubbles!

Student's Book page 18

1 Add the prefix *un–* to the start of the words below, and then use each *un–* word in a sentence.

a pleasant _____

_____

b kind _____

_____

c happy _____

_____

d seen _____

_____

e used _____

_____

f eaten _____

_____

2 Add the suffix *–able* to the words below.

a use _____	**b** believe _____
c accept _____	**d** regret _____
e adore _____	**f** do _____
g fashion _____	**h** enjoy _____

3 Pick two of your 'able' words and write a dictionary definition for each of them.

a Word: _____

Definition: _____

b Word: _____

Definition: _____

1 Write out the sentences below and add the missing capital letters and punctuation. Write 'O' by the sentences that are orders, 'Q' by the questions and 'S' by the statements.

a i like chocolate biscuits best
_____

b have you seen my football
_____

c come here at once kieran
_____

d why do you always eat the strawberry sweets first
_____

e we wanted to go to the beach with sam and mina because it was so hot
_____

f be careful or you'll wake the baby
_____

g mum says it's bedtime now
_____

h who is the fastest runner in the class
_____

i shut the door
_____

j the monster was taller than a block of flats
_____

1 Read these sentences and underline the connectives. Be careful! Some of the sentences have more than one connective!

a Marta's room was very untidy, but Lucas's room was spotless.

b I like to hum under my breath because it makes me feel happy, but it annoys my sister.

c First you turn left, and then you cross the road under the bridge.

d I like chocolate ice cream and Maria likes strawberry, but neither of us likes vanilla.

e You'll miss the bus to school, if you don't hurry up.

f Mr Osei told Jacob off because he was late to school and he had forgotten his homework.

g If you want to be a good footballer, first you need to practise hard, because there are lots of skills to learn.

2 Choose from the connectives in the box and use them to write three sentences of your own.

first	next	then	because	however	also	if

Read this story, and answer the questions below and on page 16.

"Josh! Look at that!"

Jamelia pointed to the sky behind her brother's head, and Josh spun round, his mouth open in amazement. Flapping slowly towards them, its leathery black wings stretched wide against the sky, was the most enormous dragon either of them had ever seen.

"What a beauty," whispered Josh, as he looked towards the clump of trees where the dragon was landing. "It's a Salamander Black. Have you got your phone, Jamelia? We've got to get a picture of this, or no one will ever believe it!"

Jamelia fumbled in her backpack, and a shower of objects fell out: an apple core, a torch, a small folding magic wand, a half-eaten chocolate bar and a hair band. However, there was no sign of Jamelia's phone, because she had left it behind on the bus! Jamelia looked up hopelessly, but Josh was already running across the field, and heading straight for the dragon.

a   Underline a sentence where there are commas separating items in a list.

b   Find all the sentences where commas are used to separate clauses and underline them.

c   Draw circles around all the connectives.

d Find and write out a sentence, which uses the future tense.

_____

e Find and write out a sentence, which uses the past tense.

_____

f Find and write out a sentence, which uses the present tense.

_____

g What kind of dragon have the children seen?

_____

h Are the children in the countryside, or in the town, and how do you know?

_____

_____

i Do you think the children have ever seen a dragon before? Why?

_____

_____

j What relation is Jamelia to Josh?

_____

_____

k What clues in the story tell us there is something unusual about the children?

_____

_____

l What do you think will happen next?

_____

_____

3 The power of the sea

Reading Student's Book page 27

1 Reread the poem *Old Man Ocean* on page 27 of the Student's Book.

2 Here is another poem by Russell Hoban. Read it, and then answer the questions.

a Find two words that describe how the crow flies.

_____

_____

b What kind of character do you think the crow is? Write a sentence to describe him, using your own words.

> ***The Crow***
> **by Russell Hoban**
>
>
>
> Flying loose and easy,
> where does he go
>
> Swaggering in the sky,
> what does he know,
>
> Why is he laughing, the
> carrion crow?
>
> Why is he shouting, why won't he sing,
>
> How did he steal them, whom will he bring
>
> Loaves of blue heaven under each wing?

_____

_____

c What kind of noise does the crow make?

_____

_____

d Write down the rhyming words in the poem.

_____

_____

e What do you think the poet means when he says the crow has 'Loaves of blue heaven under each wing'?

_____

_____

f What is your favourite line in the poem? Write it here:

_____

_____

g Give one reason why you like this line.

_____

_____

h Which poem do you prefer, out of *Old Man Ocean* and *The Crow*? Explain why you like it.

_____

_____

_____

Grammar   Student's Book page 28

Read the sentences below. Write 'S' at the end of the similes, and 'M' at the end of the metaphors.

a The sea is as cold as a murderer's heart. _____

b The sun was shining like a bright mirror. _____

c The moon is a silver flower. _____

d The moon rose through the sky as slowly as a butterfly. _____

e The prisoner was a caged lion, pacing up and down in his cell. _____

f The children were wriggling like tadpoles. _____

g The breeze was as delicious as strawberry ice cream. _____

h The trees are tall ships sailing across a green sea. _____

1 Read this short explanation text.

How butter is made

i) Butter is made from milk. First, the cream is separated from the milk. The cream is put into a container and shaken, or churned, until it gets thick.

ii) As it is churned, the cream gets thicker and thicker, and it also turns pale yellow. Eventually it turns solid. The solid stuff is butter! There is also some thin liquid left – this is called buttermilk.

iii) The buttermilk is poured off, leaving the butter behind.

iv) Sometimes, salt is added to the butter before it is shaped into blocks and wrapped up, ready to be sold.

2 Write the answers to these questions.

a What do you have to do to the milk before you can make butter?

_____

_____

b The text says that the cream is 'churned'. What does 'churned' mean?

_____

_____

c What is buttermilk?

_____

_____

d If you want salty butter, at what stage do you add the salt?

_____

_____

Reread the explanation text about making butter, on page 19 of this Workbook, and then answer the questions.

1 What tense is the explanation text in – past, present or future?

2 Underline all the parts of the verb 'to be' in this section:

Butter is made from milk. First, the cream is separated from the milk. The

cream is put into a container and shaken, or churned, until it gets thick.

3 Now write out the section above, changing all the present-tense verbs to past tense.

_____

_____

_____

_____

4 The verbs in these sentences are wrong! Write the sentences out correctly.

a The boys was playing cricket on the beach.

_____

b Last Wednesday the weather is very hot.

_____

c We am going to the playground after school.

_____

d In the future, we was able to live on the Moon.

_____

e I is bringing my little sister with me, because Mum and Dad am out shopping.

_____

1 Read these sentences. Underline the adjectives and circle the adverbs.

a Jake bravely dived into the deep, green pool.

b Sasha's sister Kia was small, but noisy.

c I looked both ways carefully before crossing the busy road.

d "You're acting like silly little monkeys!" said Mrs Hussein, crossly.

e The trees were waving about furiously in the strong wind.

2 Choose two adjectives and two adverbs from the box. Write a sentence using each.

| scary | happily | enormous | loudly | beautiful |
| quickly | strange | fiercely | sleepy | gloomily |

Adjectives: _____

Adverbs: _____

_____

_____

_____

_____

Student's Book page 34

1 The words from three different word families have been mixed up! Write the words into the correct spider diagrams.

> really   reappear   reality   darkest   appearance
>
> realistic   darker   surreal   apparently   disappear
>
> darkening   appearing   darkness   unreal   darkly

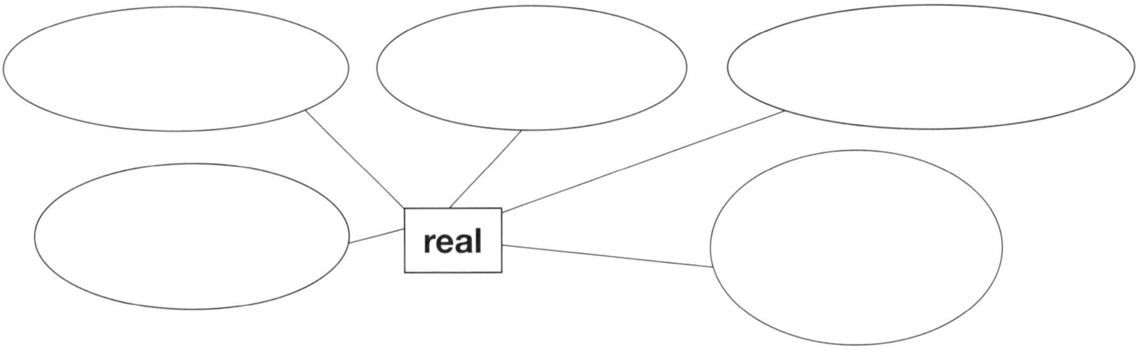

real

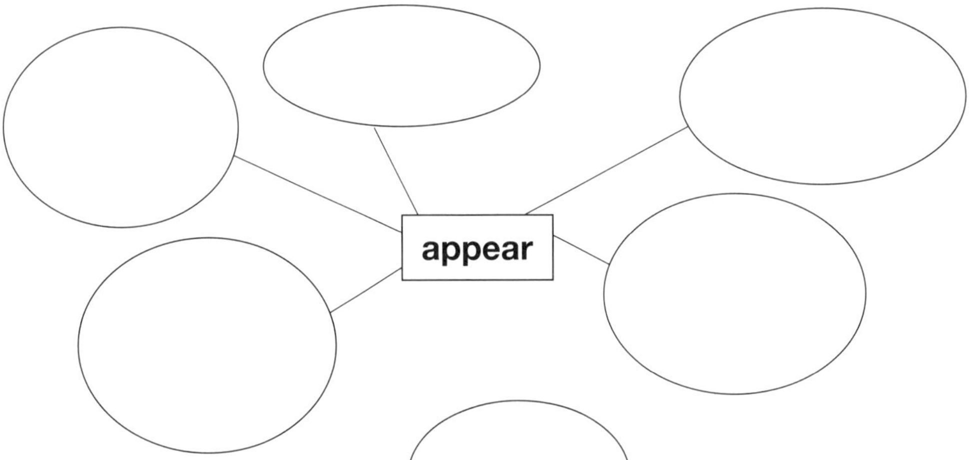

appear

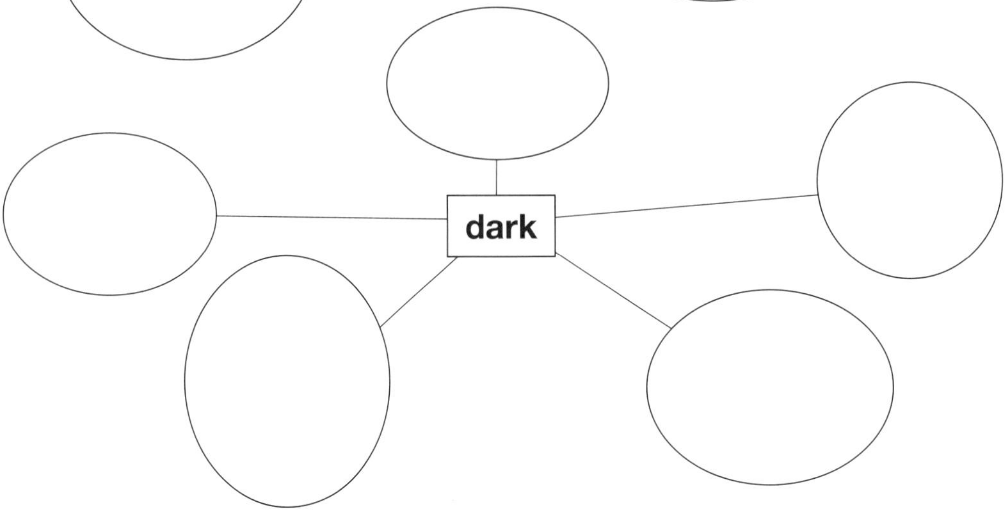

dark

2 Look at the words in the 'real' family. Write a sentence using each of them. Your sentence should show that you know what the word means!

_____

_____

_____

_____

_____

3 Fill in the word family for the root word *–able*. See if you can find at least five members of the family!

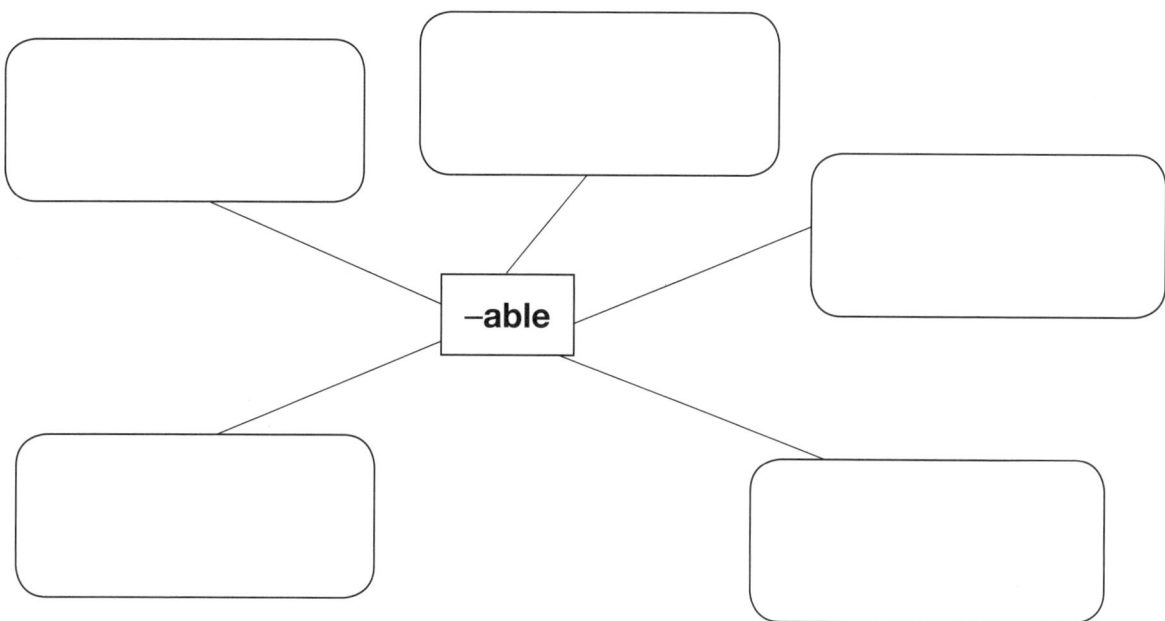

4 Other people, other places

Listening and speaking · Student's Book page 39

1 Think about the story *The Clever Farmer*. Choose one of the three main characters – the farmer, the rich man, or Shikorina the cow – and write their name in the centre of the diagram. Fill in the spider diagram with words and phrases to describe the character you have chosen. You can use the story, and your own imagination!

What the character might look like:

What the character does:

What other people think of the character:

Four good words to describe the character:

2 Would you like to meet this character? Why, or why not?

_____

_____

_____

3 Here is the first paragraph of *The Clever Farmer*. What clues does it give you about the setting of the story? Underline all the words and phrases that help you to imagine the setting.

Once there was a farmer who had fallen on hard times. His fields were full of dust and stones, his watermelons were all shrivelled up and, worst of all, he had had to get rid of all his cows. All except one, that is. The farmer couldn't bear to part with his last cow. She was the sweetest-natured animal you ever saw, and her name was Shikorina. As long as there was a bite of food in the house, the farmer shared it with Shikorina, and they managed to get by, somehow.

4 Write two sentences to describe the story setting. Make them as detailed and descriptive as you can, so that the reader can really imagine the setting!

Punctuation, speaking and reading   Student's Book page 42

1 Some of the punctuation is missing from this conversation. Add in the missing speech marks, commas and full stops!

Come on said Mum. We've got to go shopping

Oh! moaned Ali Do we have to?

Yes said Mum. We've got no food left in the house

All right then said Ali. I'll go and get my coat

Good said Mum If you help with the shopping, I'll take you swimming later

2 Read the speech bubbles. Write what the cat and bird are saying as direct speech. Don't forget to add 'said the cat' and 'said the bird' – and don't forget the punctuation!

Come back. I only want to play with you.

No thank you! I know what your games are like!

_____

_____

_____

_____

_____

_____

Punctuation Student's Book page 43

1 Add the missing apostrophes to these sentences.

a Jakes toys were all over the floor.

b The childrens faces were covered in chocolate.

c The dragons cave was dark and damp. (Only one dragon.)

d Maras job was to fill up her pet hamsters water bowl. (More than one hamster.)

e The girls bicycles had flat tyres. (More than one girl.)

f Rachel looked everywhere for Sams lost bear.

g The mens changing room was very crowded.

h We scattered the chickens food all over the yard. (More than one chicken)

i The rabbits leg was broken.

j My mobile phones battery is dead.

2 Write a sentence about each of these things. Don't forget possessive apostrophes!

a The football belonging to Padma:

_____

b The books belonging to the children:

_____

c The teeth belonging to the ogre:

_____

d The eggs belonging to the ducks:

_____

Writing Student's Book page 47

1 Underline the adjectives in these sentences. Then write the sentences out again, changing each adjective into a stronger one. (For example, if the adjective was 'sad', you might change it to 'miserable'.)

a Kamila was happy to see her friends.

_____

b There was a small kitten asleep in the chair.

_____

c A large dinosaur suddenly burst out of the wood.

_____

d Tom was cold, so he put on his coat.

_____

e We enjoyed our ice creams, because it was a hot day.

_____

f The old giant was angry.

_____

2 Write out these sentences again, and add an adverb to each one.

a Jack skipped home.

_____

b The giant roared at us.

_____

c Mum hugged me.

_____

d I ran downstairs.

_____

e An owl flew past.

_____

Spelling   Student's Book pages 47–48

1 How many syllables are in each of these words? Write the number next to each word.

a happily _____   **b** correct _____

c kicking _____   **d** somebody _____

e underneath _____   **f** beautiful _____

2 One word in each of these sentences is spelt incorrectly. Write the word correctly at the end of the line.

a Sumbody must have taken my book. _____

b I feel happy wenever I hear that song. _____

c My fayvorite meal is pizza. _____

d Evryone makes mistakes sometimes. _____

e It's a byootiful day. _____

3 The wrong homophones have been used in these sentences. Cross out the wrong ones and write the correct spelling above the word.

a I saw wear Mum put the cakes.

b I've got two much homework too do.

c Ben is good at reading and righting.

d I wood love to go swimming.

e It's a long weigh to Kuala Lumpur.

f Dad is knot hear this evening.

4 Write a sentence using each of these homophone words correctly.

a seen _____

b scene _____

c sum _____

d some _____

e here _____

f hear _____

Grammar   Student's Book page 48

1 Rewrite these sentences, putting them into the past tense.

a I am excited because it is my turn to go down the water slide.

_____

b Priti is wearing her best blue sari.

_____

c We are walking into town.

_____

d Michael and Ruben are arguing again.

_____

2 Turn the past tense sentences into the future tense, and the future tense sentences into the past tense.

a Dad was in New York.

_____

b I will be nine on Saturday.

_____

c Sabah and Emily will be the winners.

_____

d We were happy to see Grandma.

_____

3 Change these sentences from the present tense to the past tense. Be careful! Some of the verbs are irregular!

a Mum becomes very cross when we get mud on the carpet.

_____

b I write my name carefully.

_____

c The dragon flies over the rooftops.

_____

d Ruth and Jacob come swimming with us.

_____

e A large parcel stands in the corner of the room.

_____

5 The only problem is ...

Reading Student's Book pages 53–54

1 Read these sentences from *Meeting Mr Faulkner*. Underline the adjectives, and draw a circle round the verbs. Be careful! Not every sentence has an adjective – and some have more than one adjective.

a He wasn't a posh banker, though he did have the most enormous box of chocolates tucked under one arm.

b I sidled out of the shadow.

c They were those rich, dark, expensive, chocolate-coated cream mints.

d Jude rushed upstairs, clutching her booty to her chest.

e Jude came thundering downstairs.

f He tipped the enraptured Floss into Jude's arms, and ambled past me with a nod.

2 Draw a line to link the verbs that are similar in meaning. Draw a circle round the verb that is the strongest. The first one has been done for you.

walk	chatter
warble	slump
sprint	eat
gobble	run
guffaw	plod
smile	laugh
sit	beam
talk	sing

1 Underline the adverbs in these sentences. Draw a circle round the verb that goes with each adverb.

a I stupidly put the ice cream in the oven instead of in the freezer.

b Jonathan jumped around excitedly.

c Samira looked sadly out of the window.

d "Yippee! We've got my favourite food for dinner!" yelped Mica delightedly.

e Rafiq clumsily dropped his glass on the floor.

f Miserably, Santi plodded home.

g "Never mind, Michael," Ella whispered softly.

h Mr Wong loudly shouted, "Go back to your seats at once!"

2 Write these sentences out again, adding an adverb.

a I trod on my best pen and broke it.

_____

b I drank the chocolate milkshake.

_____

c Benji ran all the way home.

_____

d Sasha yawned and lay down in bed.

_____

e "I told you not to tell anyone!" said Anna.

_____

3 Write a sentence about how you eat your breakfast in the morning. Don't forget to use an adverb – and make it as strong and vivid as you can!

_____

_____

1 All the punctuation has fallen off these sentences! Rewrite them with capital letters and punctuation. At the end of each sentence, write 'S' if it's a statement, 'Q' if it's a question or 'O' if it's an order.

a dont let me see you do that ever again ☐

_____

b how many sweets have you got left ☐

_____

c daniels favourite red top had holes in it ☐

_____

d when did you first come to this school ☐

_____

e be careful when you are using knives ☐

_____

f i have always wanted to visit barcelona ☐

_____

2 Write a question, statement and order of your own!

- **Question:** _____

- **Statement:** _____

- **Order:** _____

Read this piece of text. The author has forgotten the paragraph breaks! Draw a mark like this // to show where the paragraphs need to go.

"Come on, Charlie," said Maya. "We're going to miss the bus!" "Hang on!" snapped Charlie. "Give me a moment – I'm nearly ready." "Well," said Maya, "I'm going to the bus stop. I'll see you there – if the bus doesn't get there before you do!" Maya skipped off down the road to the bus stop. Her friend Patsy was already waiting there. "Hi, Patsy!" yelled

Maya. "Are you going to the match too?" "Of course!" said Patsy. "I wouldn't miss it – it's not every day that your team gets to the final!" Just then, Charlie came running up, panting and puffing. "I think you forgot something, Maya," he gasped. He was waving a pair of tickets for the match. "We won't get far without these!"

1 These words all contain the letter string *ea* – but these letters do not always make the same sound! Write each *ea* word in the correct circle.

beach	dead	bread	breakfast	seat	deal	healthy
heal	meadow	steal	leaves	stealth	feast	feather
steam	reach	thread	team	bead	great	tread
spread	treat	peak	leather	break		

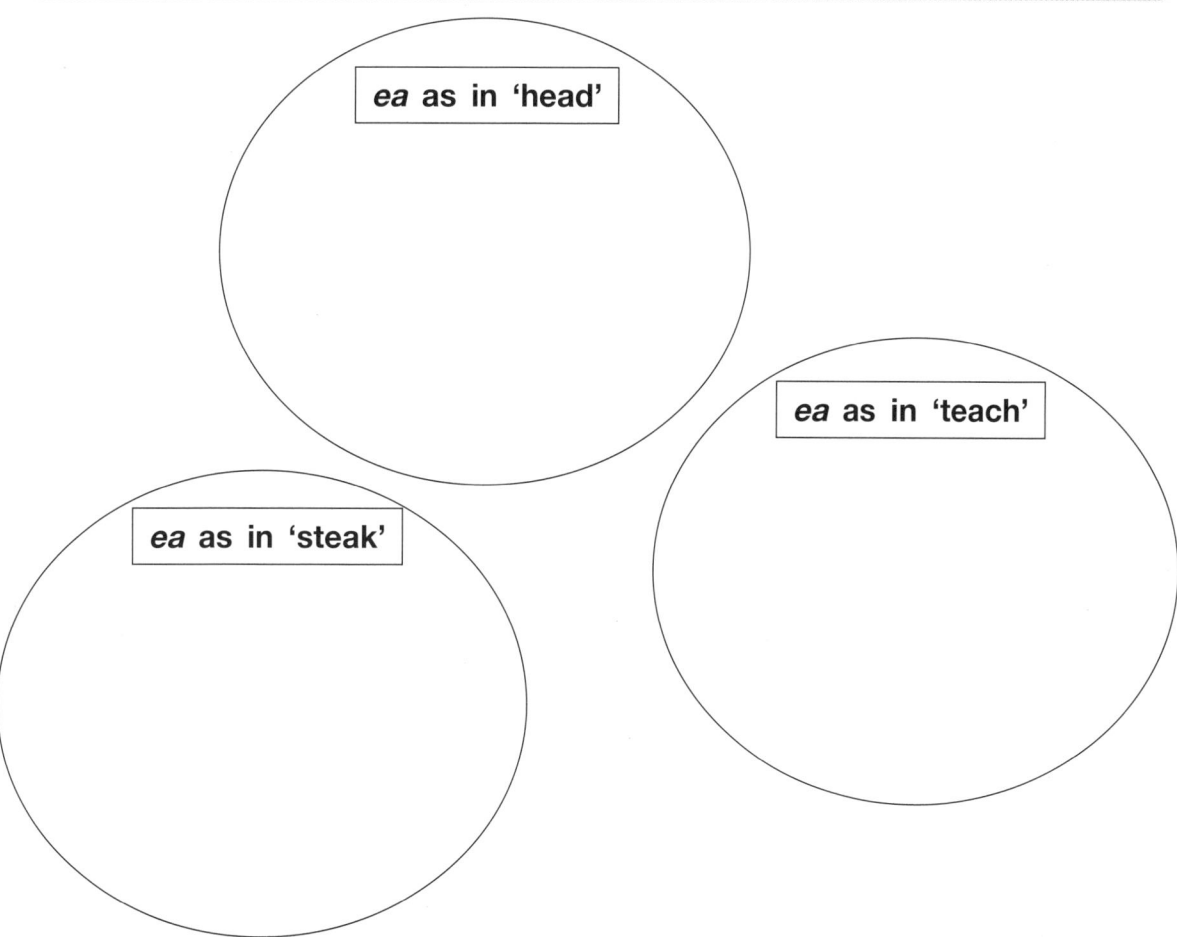

ea as in 'head'

ea as in 'teach'

ea as in 'steak'

2 Now choose one word from each circle and write a sentence using that word.

a *ea* as in 'head': _____

b *ea* as in 'steak': _____

c *ea* as in 'teach': _____

Read these sentences. Write a more interesting word to replace the underlined word in each.

a   It was <u>great</u> when our team won the football match. _____

b   The flowers in Ravi's garden looked <u>nice</u>. _____

c   Maddie got lost in the <u>big</u> shop. _____

d   I saw a <u>little</u> mouse running across the floor. _____

e   Even though he was wearing his coat, Jamie was <u>cold</u>. _____

f   Paula <u>shouted</u> to me across the crowded room. _____

g   Jerome <u>went</u> along the road. _____

h   I <u>like</u> chocolate cake. _____

i   I <u>hate</u> spinach. _____

j   The baby <u>cried</u> loudly. _____

6 Making the headlines

Reading, listening and speaking Student's Book pages 63–64

1 Reread the newspaper article, *Malala's award*. Jot notes on this mind map as you read.

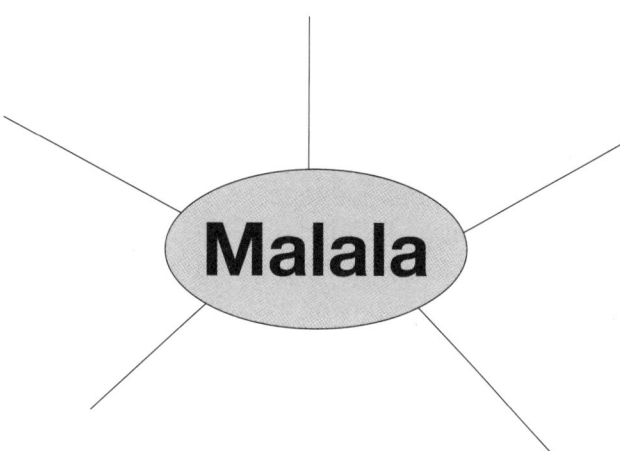

Malala

2 Now use your mind map to help you write a paragraph about Malala. Aim to write at least one sentence for each point on your mind map.

_____

_____

_____

_____

_____

_____

_____

1 Read this short newspaper article, then answer the questions.

NEW FROG SPECIES FOUND

by Charles Matthews, Science correspondent

June 2015: Brazilian scientists have discovered seven new species of tiny frogs, high up in the remote mountains on Brazil's southern coastline.

They have evolved with fewer fingers and toes than other frogs, and they do not go through a tadpole stage. Instead, they come out of their eggs like fully-formed adults. They can even survive out of ponds and rivers, because they are good at absorbing water from the ground through their skins. Most amazingly of all, the largest of the seven species grows to just 13 millimetres long!

Professor Marcio Pie, the lead scientist on the project, said that he had climbed more mountains than he can remember, in search of the frogs. "It was really exhausting!" he told us. "But there was always the feeling of anticipation and curiosity about what the new species might look like."

2 Find the following newspaper features in the article.

- Draw a ring around the headline.

- Draw a wavy line under the journalist's name.

- Draw a straight line under the sentence that sums up the key point of the article.

- Draw a zigzag line under a sentence that grabs the reader's interest.

- Draw a dotted line under a quotation.

1 Look at the root words below. Add *–ed* and *–ing* to the word. The first one has been done for you.

a park Spelling: parked, parking   **b danc** Spelling: _____

c try Spelling: _____   **d jog** Spelling: _____

e ste Spelling: _____   **f stamp** Spelling: _____

g carry Spelling: _____   **h slope** Spelling: _____

i gli Spelling: _____   **j bury** Spelling: _____

k dri Spelling: _____   **l chang** Spelling: _____

m jump Spelling: _____   **n pi** Spelling: _____

2 Read these sentences. The *–ed* and *–ing* words have been spelt wrongly! Cross them out and write the correct spellings.

a Harry walkied slowly to school _____.

b I was hurriing so I triped up on the stairs _____.

c Selma placd her cup carefully on the table _____.

d Nadim had trouble liftying his heavy bag off the floor _____.

e My cousin is getting marryed next week _____.

f I voteed for Carlo to be Class President _____.

g My grandma knited me a purple and pink cardigan _____.

h We had fun slideing down the water slide _____.

1 Add the missing commas to these sentences.

a My dad who goes out for a run every morning is training for a 10-kilometre race.

b The sky which had been so sunny in the morning was now covered in thick clouds.

c I just nibbled one of the cookies although Mum had told me not to because they looked so delicious.

d Ali's hair which hadn't been cut for a long time was dangling in his eyes.

e I felt very cold even though it was August so I put on my thick coat.

2 Now think of a phrase of your own to add between the commas in these sentences. Say it out loud before you write it, to make sure it makes sense.

a The children, _____ , shouted happily as they went on the swings.

b Dad's car, _____ , is extremely old and rusty.

c My favourite dinner, _____ , was waiting for me when I got home.

d My teacher Mrs Nosarka, _____ , gave us a maths test.

e Mariam's best pen, _____ , seems to have gone missing.

1 Read this set of instructions. The connectives are missing. Choose the best connective from the box to fill each gap. You may need to use some more than once.

first	next	and	so	then	finally	now

Make a hoop game!

What you need:

five paper plates

the cardboard tube from a roll of kitchen paper

a pencil

a mug or glass

a pair of scissors

sticky tape

brightly coloured paints or felt-tip pens

What to do:

a _____, take a paper plate _____ put the mug or glass down in the middle of it. Draw round the mug or glass _____ there is a circle in the middle of the plate.

b _____, cut the circle out of the middle of the plate _____ you are left with a ring.

c _____ do the same with three of the other plates.

d Colour or paint the rings using bright colours.

e _____, take the cardboard tube _____ stick it to the last plate with sticky tape, _____ it will stand upright.

f _____ throw your rings _____ see how many you can get to land over the tube!

2 Reread the instructions. Draw a circle round all the command verbs (like 'make', 'do' etc.).

41

7 Inventions

Spelling Student's Book pages 77–78

1 Write out these animal names in alphabetical order. Remember – if there are two words starting with the same letters, you need to look at the first different letters of each word, to decide which comes first in the alphabet.

kangaroo	_____
elephant	_____
lizard	_____
mouse	_____
hippopotamus	_____
anteater	_____
lion	_____
rabbit	_____
koala	_____
elk	_____
hare	_____
antelope	_____

2 Write these surnames in the order they would appear in the telephone directory (alphabetical order).

Patel	_____
Burroughs	_____
Wang	_____
Howard	_____
Lau	_____
Peters	_____
Latimer	_____
Bains	_____
Smithson	_____
Persaud	_____
Khan	_____
Hussain	_____

3 These children are lining up in alphabetical order. The child on the left is called Anna. Make up a name for each of the other children. Remember that they need to be in alphabetical order!

Anna _____ _____ _____ _____ _____

1 Find and write down four reasons why A. Baxter thinks the Internet is a great invention.

_____

_____

_____

_____

2 Why does A. Baxter think email is useful?

_____

_____

3 What was the date the letter was written?

_____

_____

4 Do you think A. Baxter's letter is convincing? Why, or why not?

_____

_____

5 What do *you* think is the best invention ever? Explain why you think this. Give at least two reasons.

_____

_____

_____

_____

6 Find and write down three connectives used in the letter.

_____

_____

1 Change these sentences to the past tense:

a Orla will win the running race.

_____

b I am glad to see Ella.

_____

2 Change these sentences to the future tense:

a We went to the beach on Saturday.

_____

b They are painting Grace's bedroom pink.

_____

3 Change these sentences to the present tense:

a Janine will see the three kittens.

_____

b Mum went to the shops.

_____

4 Read this story. Draw a circle round sentences in the present tense, a straight line under sentences in the past tense, and a wiggly line under sentences in the future.

It was Saturday afternoon, and I was bored. Well, can you blame me? Nothing interesting will ever happen in our house. I had played all my games and read all my books, and I had nothing to do.

Suddenly, there was a knock on my bedroom door. I got a shock!

"Who is that? What do you want?"

I crept to the door and opened it. You will never guess what I saw!

1 Add the end-of-sentence punctuation to these sentences.

a I'm so glad you're coming round to our house to play

b Do you like chocolate

c It's my dad's birthday on Wednesday

d My teacher's name is Mrs Ismael

e There's a wasp on your arm

f I've never felt so happy

g There's a dragon in the playground

h How many sisters do you have

i Dad's favourite colour is green

j On Saturday we went to the shops

2 Write a question, an exclamation and a statement (ending in a full stop). Remember to use the right punctuation at the end of each sentence!

- **Question:** _____

- **Exclamation:** _____

- **Statement:** _____

Student's Book page 85

1 Draw a line to link these nouns with the verbs they come from. The first has been done for you.

excitement   operate

celebration   decide

management   divert

connection   excite

agreement   define

decision   celebrate

definition   manage

argument   educate

diversion   measure

measurement   connect

education   agree

operation   argue

2 Write the verb that each of these nouns comes from.

a **announcement**   _____

b **contradiction**   _____

c **punishment**   _____

d **demonstration**   _____

e **entertainment**   _____

f **co-operation**   _____

g **encouragement**   _____

3 Write the noun that comes from these verbs. (Clue: the nouns end in either *–ion* or *–ment*.)

a decorate _____

b possess _____

c assess _____

d navigate _____

e pay _____

f irritate _____

g announce _____

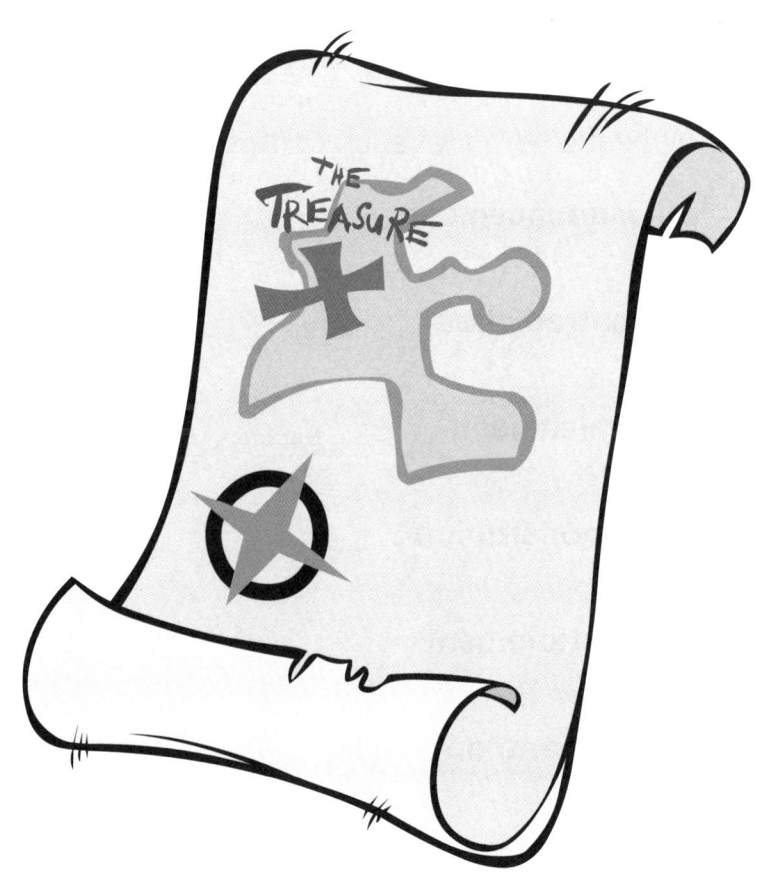

8 Putting on a show

1 Read these sentences. Draw a circle round the powerful verbs.

a Charles stomped crossly out of the room.

b Maxine grabbed the plate and hurled it out of the window.

c "How dare you do that?" Mum thundered.

d Romy's cat, Alexia, slunk in through the door.

e "It wasn't my fault," muttered Sam.

f The hippopotamus wallowed in the soft river mud.

g Eight pigeons strutted towards us, looking for food.

h I yelled at my brother because he used my pens without asking.

2 Add adverbs (like 'sadly' or 'happily') in the brackets below, to show how the character would say the words.

a **ALICE:** (_____) I can't believe you just did that!

b **MUM:** (_____) Never mind, darling, it'll all be over soon.

c **GRAN:** (_____) Well, in my day, children had to play quietly!

d **MR ABAJO:** (_____) Class Four! Come back here this instant!

e **ASIF:** (_____) I wish we could go to Fab Towers theme park!

f **BARNEY:** (_____) I'm only coming if Jake can come too.

g **FATIMA:** (_____) Oh! I didn't see you standing there, Selma!

h **DAD:** (_____) Hurry up, boys! You'll be late for school!

Spelling — Student's Book page 94

1 All the words in the box can be turned into their opposites, by adding one of the prefixes *im–*, *in–*, *ir–* or *il–* at the start. Write the correct prefix in front of each word.

_____visible   _____logical   _____credible   _____possible

_____relevant   _____mature   _____correct

2 Now use these words to complete this crossword.

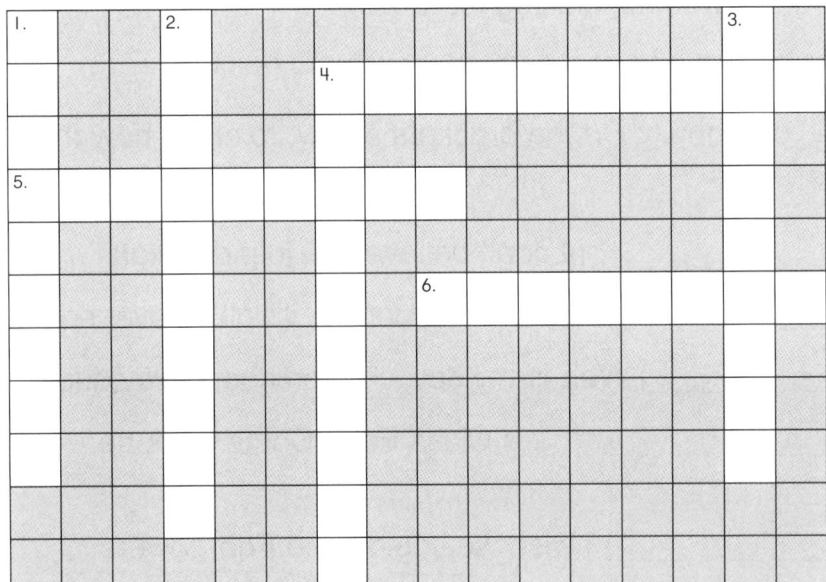

Clues

Down

1 You can't see it!

2 It just can't be done.

3 It's not right.

4 I don't believe it!

Across

4 That's nothing to do with it – it's _____.

5 There's no logic to that!

6 Act your age – you're so _____!

1 Fill the gaps below with either *–ible* or *–able*.

a After working hard all day in the garden, Grandad was asleep in a comfort_____ chair.

b The tiny kittens looked ador_____.

c I'll never get all my homework done tonight – it's imposs_____!

d James ate his dry, stale sandwich, but it wasn't very enjoy_____.

e My little brother's handwriting is absolutely terr_____.

f The sunset was an incred_____ shade of purple, with pink clouds.

g If poss_____, I'd like to go to the park after school.

h The painting on the museum wall was very valu_____.

i The weather today is really horr_____.

j Emma's family have an old car that keeps breaking down – it's not very reli_____.

k I bought a big bag of sweets at the market for a very reason_____ price.

l I'm feeling much better now – my spots are nearly invis_____.

2 Write out these words on page 51 in the order you would find them in the dictionary. Then write a definition of each word. Use your dictionary if you need to!

anger	bath	angrily	balance	submarine
subtle	brim	beetle	alligator	seahorse
seaside	trainers	flying	triangle	fairground
triple	valiant	valuable		

Word: _____ Definition: _____

Word: _____ Definition: _____

Word: _____ Definition: _____

Word: _____ Definition: _____

Word: _____ Definition: _____

Word: _____ Definition: _____

Word: _____ Definition: _____

Word: _____ Definition: _____

Word: _____ Definition: _____

Word: _____ Definition: _____

Word: _____ Definition: _____

Word: _____ Definition: _____

Word: _____ Definition: _____

Word: _____ Definition: _____

Word: _____ Definition: _____

Word: _____ Definition: _____

Word: _____ Definition: _____

Word: _____ Definition: _____

9 Imaginary worlds

Listening and speaking Student's Book pages 98–99

Look at the words in the box below. Add each of the words to the correct list.

scientist	walk	guess	scenic	scent	lamb	debt
foreign	knew	resign	chalk	knife	scenery	kneel
hymn	crumb	know	solemn	listen	campaign	
jostle	talk	wriggle	rustle	wrinkle	thistle	disguise
guest	wrap	knot	wreckage	half	comb	calf

Silent c
science
scene
ascend
_____
_____
_____
_____

Silent b
doubt
bomb
_____
_____
_____
_____

Silent g
sign
gnome
gnat
_____
_____
_____

Silent k
knight
knee
_____
_____
_____
_____

Silent n
autumn
column
_____
_____

Silent w
wreck
wrong
_____
_____
_____
_____

Silent t
bristle
castle
_____
_____
_____
_____

Silent u
guitar
guilty
_____
_____
_____
_____

Silent i
calm
balm
_____
_____
_____
_____

Student's Book page 100

1 Underline the verbs in these pieces of dialogue.
At the end of each sentence, write 'past', 'present' or 'future'.

a "I am going to count up to ten, and then I will
come and find you!" _____

b "How many biscuits did you eat?" _____

c "It is Dad's turn to cook dinner today." _____

d "Gran said I could take Fluffy for a walk." _____

e "My favourite colour is red." _____

f "We are going to go to America on holiday next year." _____

2 Add the missing verbs into these pieces of dialogue. The first one has been
done for you.

a "Molly <u>is going to</u> come round to my house today." (future)

b "We _____ down to the park after school." (future)

c "I hope there _____ pasta for tea." (future)

d "David _____ the winner of the running race." (past)

e "When I _____ little, my favourite toy _____
a bear." (past)

f "We _____ a big chocolate cake on my birthday." (past)

g "_____ you ready to go out?" (present)

h "Mum _____ calling you!" (present)

i "My favourite team _____ Real Madrid." (present)

Grammar | Student's Book page 102

1 This is meant to be an exciting opening for a story. Unfortunately, the writer has used some very boring verbs! Cross out the boring verbs and write a more exciting verb above each one.

Jamie went down from the spaceship on to the planet surface. He looked around him. When he saw a herd of big aliens coming towards him, he shouted out. He went back to the spaceship, but it was too late. The aliens had seen him, and they went towards the spaceship.

2 Add some interesting adverbs to these sentences.

   a The aliens flew _____ across the desert towards us.

   b Their eyes glinted _____ in the light of the fire.

   c The space monster roared _____.

   d The captain shouted at us _____.

3 Now add some interesting descriptive adjectives to these sentences.

   a The herd of _____ aliens was thundering towards Jamie.

   b Their _____ mouths were bristling

   with _____ teeth.

   c Jamie could see their _____ claws reaching out towards him.

1 Add the missing punctuation to these pieces of dialogue.

a Are you ready to land on the planet surface asked the Captain

b Yes said Jenna I think I'm as ready as I'll ever be

c Good said the captain This is going to be a very difficult mission

d I'm sure I'm ready for it said Jenna

e Don't forget your invisibility shield said the Captain You're going to need it

2 Imagine that when Jenna lands on the planet, she finds a nest of alien dinosaurs. They are only babies, but they are huge! Then she hears a rumbling sound and looks up. The babies' mother is running towards her! Write the conversation she has with the Captain when she radios back to the spaceship for help. Write at least two things for each character to say, and don't forget the punctuation!

Jenna: _____

_____

Captain: _____

_____

Jenna: _____

_____

Captain: _____

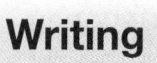

Fill in the boxes below to help you plan a non-rhyming poem about an imaginary creature.

1 What kind of creature will you write about? It could be an imaginary creatureyou have read about (like an ogre, a dragon or an elf) or it could be one youhave made up yourself!

Write the creature's name here.

_____

2 Write some notes in the boxes to help you describe the creature. Think of some good descriptive verbs, adverbs and adjectives that you could use in the poem.

It looks like ...	**It sounds like ...**

It moves like ...	**It makes me feel ...**

3 What does the creature do? Write some notes about what might happen in the poem.

> **First the creature …**
>
>
> **Then it …**
>
>
> **At the end of the poem it …**

4 Can you think of any similes (like 'as dark as night') or metaphors (like 'its face was a white moon') to describe your creature? Write them here.

5 Can you think of a strong word or phrase that would make a good repeating refrain for your poem? Write it here.

6 Now write a first draft of your poem in your notebook or on a separate piece of paper. The way a poem sounds is very important. Say the words out loud to yourself, to make sure that they sound good.

7 Make any changes you need to and then write out the whole poem in your best handwriting. You could add a drawing of your imaginary creature!

Student's Book page 106

1 Draw a line between the homophone pairs below.

eye	wear
bear	there
by	write
deer	hole
four	buy
hour	I
whole	our
male	one
won	some
right	sea
see	bare
sum	dear
their	for
too	mail
where	two

2 Pick the correct homophone from the lists above, to fill each of the gaps in these sentences.

a _____ are you going?

b I left my bag over _____.

c Lara can _____ very neatly.

d Our team _____ the obstacle race.

e We've got chicken noodle soup _____ dinner.

f The postman has just delivered the _____.

g Would you like _____ juice?

h The little boat was floating on the _____.

i I finished reading the _____ book in one day.

j I went to the park and Ahmed came _____.